Solve the picture sums and match them to their answers.

9

4

2

5

Subtract and solve the sums

$\begin{array}{r} 6 \\ -\ 2 \\ \hline \end{array}$	$\begin{array}{r} 5 \\ -\ 5 \\ \hline \end{array}$	$\begin{array}{r} 9 \\ -\ 2 \\ \hline \end{array}$
$\begin{array}{r} 7 \\ -\ 2 \\ \hline \end{array}$	$\begin{array}{r} 7 \\ -\ 5 \\ \hline \end{array}$	$\begin{array}{r} 8 \\ -\ 2 \\ \hline \end{array}$
$\begin{array}{r} 4 \\ -\ 1 \\ \hline \end{array}$	$\begin{array}{r} 3 \\ -\ 2 \\ \hline \end{array}$	$\begin{array}{r} 8 \\ -\ 8 \\ \hline \end{array}$
$\begin{array}{r} 3 \\ -\ 1 \\ \hline \end{array}$	$\begin{array}{r} 8 \\ -\ 1 \\ \hline \end{array}$	$\begin{array}{r} 5 \\ -\ 4 \\ \hline \end{array}$

Subtract and solve the sums

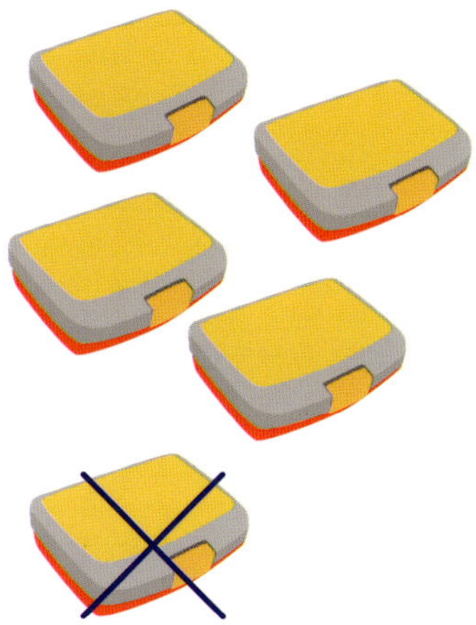

5
- 1
______

8
- 5
______

6
- 5
______

4
- 2
______

5
- 2
______

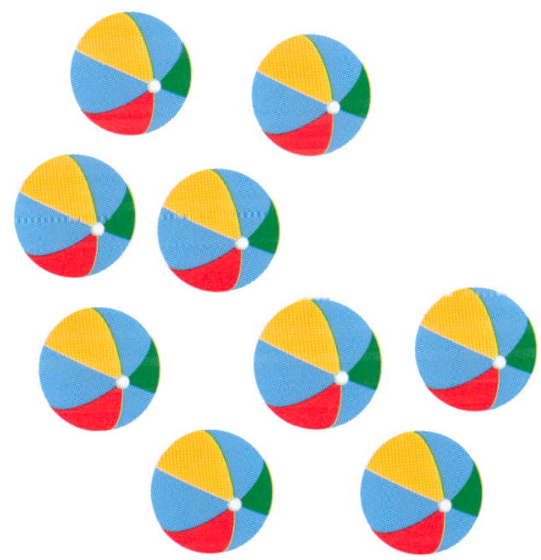

9
- 5
______

3
- 2
______

6
- 4
______

Solve the picture sums. Choose the correct answer and write it in the circle.

2 | 1 | 3

4 | 6 | 5

9 | 5 | 7

6 | 7 | 9

4 | 8 | 6

1 | 4 | 3

11 | 12 | 13

6 | 8 | 5

Solve the sums and match them to the answer in the middle.

$5 - 3$ = ____	7	8 - 1
$8 - 1$ = ____	3	6 - 3
$6 - 3$ = ____	2	5 - 3

Add the carrots and write the answer in the box.

 +  = ☐

 +  = ☐

 +  = ☐

Solve the problems

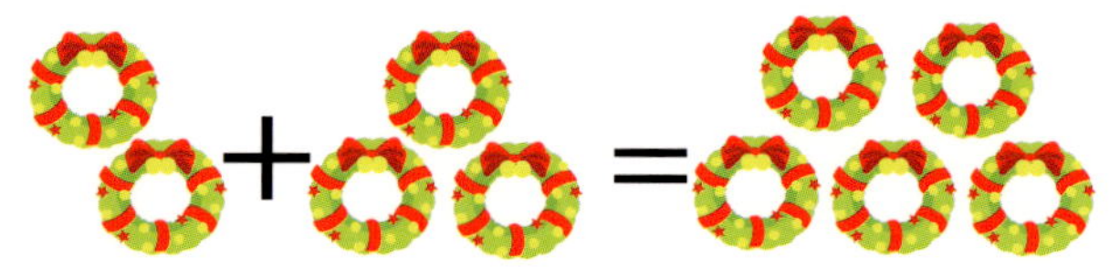

2 + 3 =

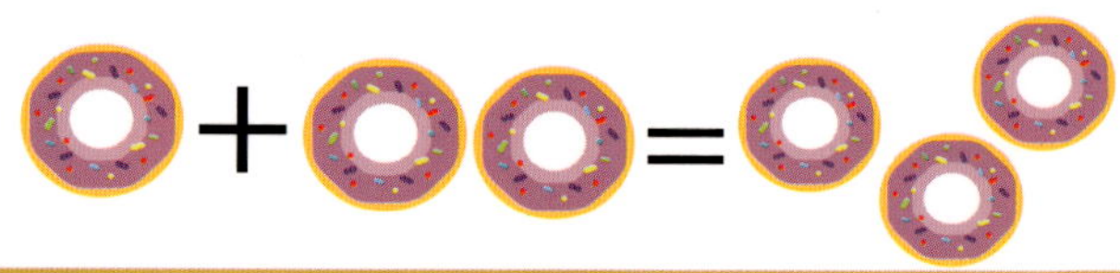

1 + 2 =

3 + 4 =

4 + 5 =

5 + 2 =

5 + 1 =

4 + 4 =

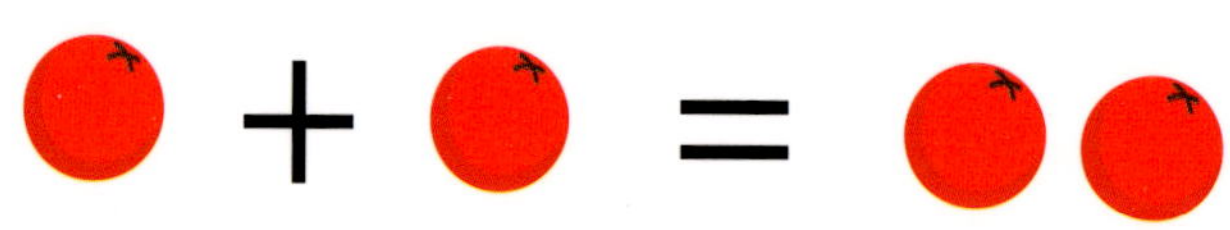

1 + 1 =

Solve the picture sums and circle the correct answer.

6

4

8

5

4

2

8

9

7

3

2

4

Add the candies and write the answer in the given space.

Solve the problems

Solve the sums

Add and write the answers

8 + 2 = ___

6 + 6 = ___

Solve and match the correct answer

5 + 1	7
4 + 3	4
6 + 3	6
2 + 2	9

Solve the problems

2 - 1 =

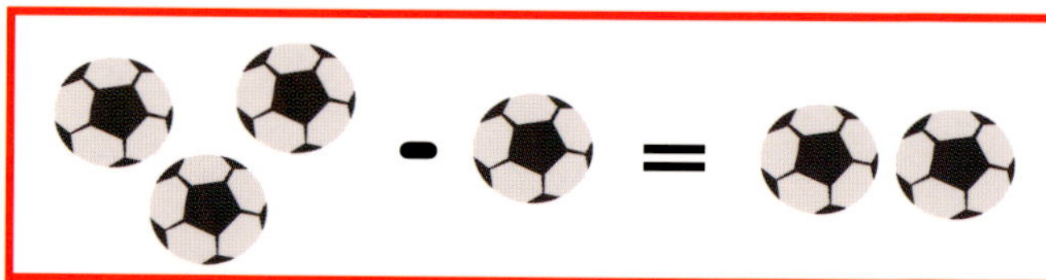

3 - 1 =

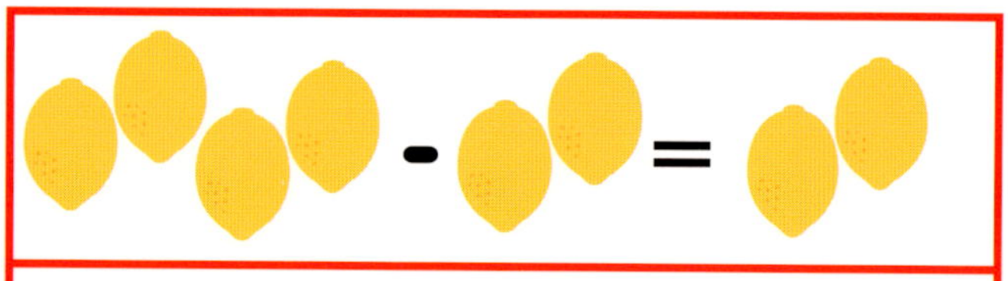

4 - 2 =

5 - 4 =

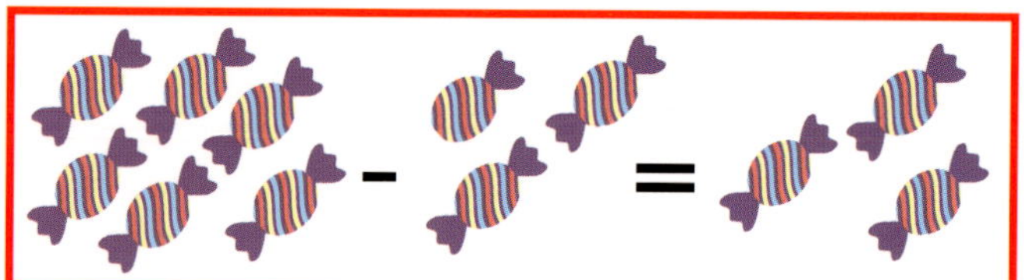

6 - 3 =

7 - 5 =

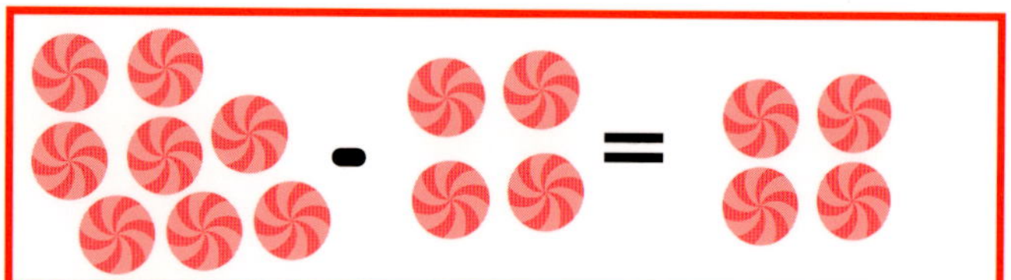

8 - 4 =

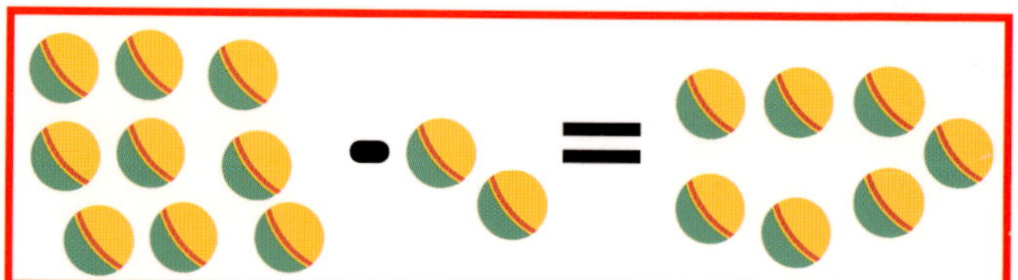

9 - 2 =

Solve the subtraction sums

12 - 5 = 7

6 - 2

9 - 1

4 - 2

9 - 5

3 - 1

8 - 4

14 - 6

Solve and match the correct answer

9 - 5

6 - 3

7 - 2

4 - 3

3

5

1

4

Solve the sums and write the answers

$$\begin{array}{r} 9 \\ +\ 4 \\ \hline \end{array}$$

$$\begin{array}{r} 5 \\ +\ 0 \\ \hline \end{array}$$

$$\begin{array}{r} 5 \\ +\ 2 \\ \hline \end{array}$$

$$\begin{array}{r} 6 \\ +\ 2 \\ \hline \end{array}$$

$$\begin{array}{r} 9 \\ +\ 7 \\ \hline \end{array}$$

Subtract and write the answers

7 - 3 = 4 ✓

4 - 2 = ____

6 - 3 = ____

3 - 1 = ____

Solve the sums, choose the correct answer and write it in the given space.

1. 5 + 2 = ____ ○ 7 ○ 9 ○ 4

3. 1 + 1 = ____ ○ 1 ○ 2 ○ 3

2. 3 + 6 = ____ ○ 1 ○ 9 ○ 2

4. 7 + 2 = ____ ○ 4 ○ 1 ○ 9

Solve the problems

6 - 2 ◯ 6 - 4 ◯ 4 - 1 ◯ 4 - 2 ◯

8 - 1 ◯ 5 - 3 ◯ 9 - 4 ◯ 2 - 2 ◯

Solve the sums.

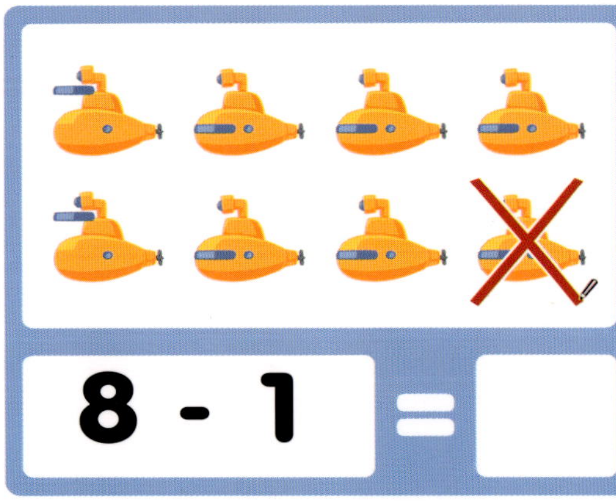

8 - 1 = ☐

3 - 1 = ☐

4 - 2 = ☐

9 - 2 = ☐

Use the picture code to solve the sums and write the answers.

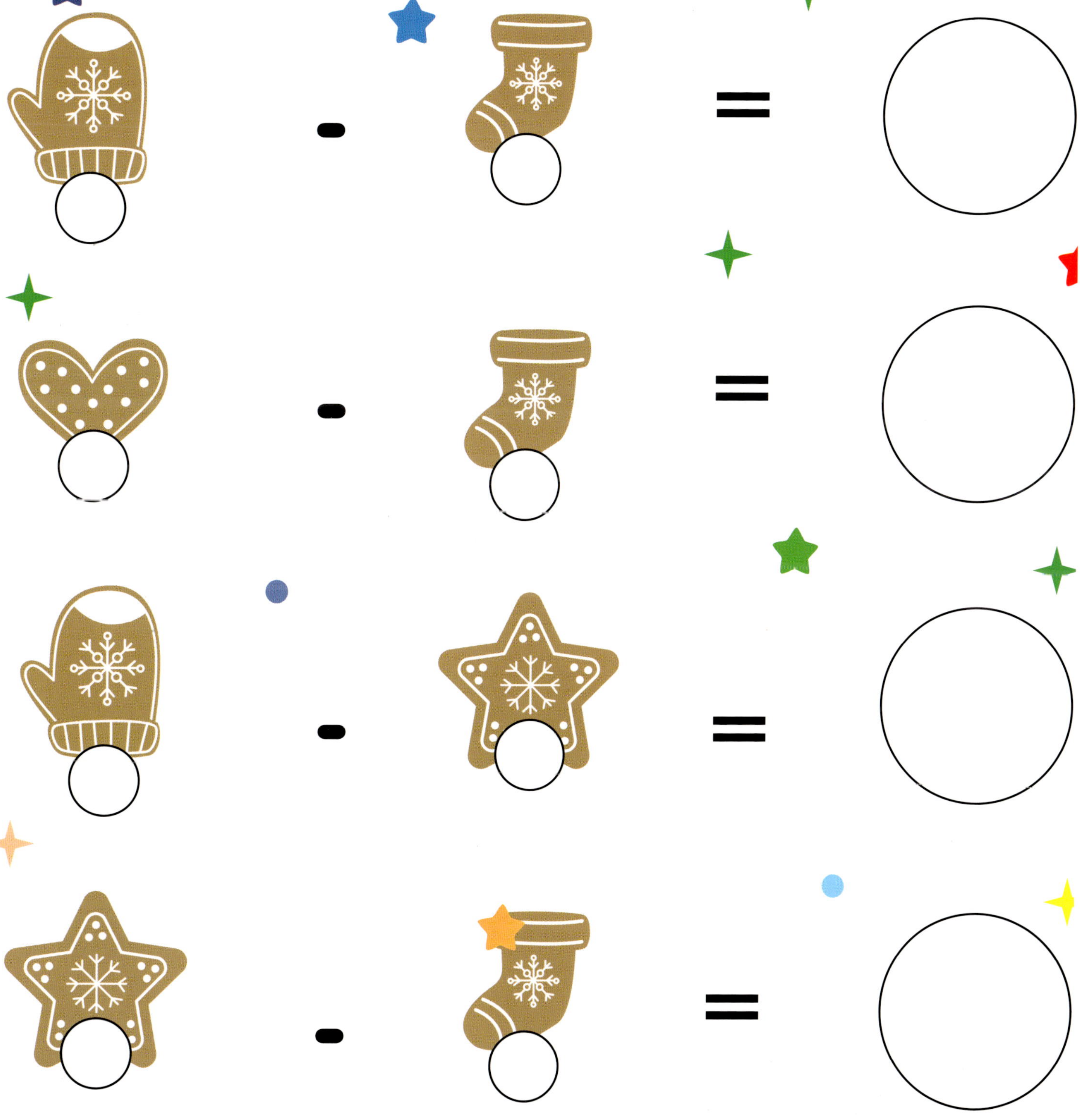

Use the picture code to solve the sums and write the answers.

 = 1  = 2  = 3  = 4

 +  =

 +  =

 +  =

 +  =